Brands We Know

Amazon

By Sara Green

Bellwether Media • Minneapolis, MN

Jump into the cockpit and take flight with Pilot books. Your journey will take you on high-energy adventures as you learn about all that is wild, weird, fascinating, and fun!

This is not an official Amazon book. It is not approved by or connected with Amazon.com, Inc.

This edition first published in 2018 by Bellwether Media, Inc.

No part of this publication may be reproduced in whole or in part without written permission of the publisher.
For information regarding permission, write to Bellwether Media, Inc.,
Attention: Permissions Department,
5357 Penn Avenue South, Minneapolis, MN 55419.

Library of Congress Cataloging-in-Publication Data

Names: Green, Sara, 1964- author.
Title: Amazon / by Sara Green.
Description: Minneapolis, MN : Bellwether Media, Inc., 2018. | Series: Pilot.
  Brands We Know | Audience: Ages 7-13. | Audience: Grades 3-8. | Includes
  bibliographical references and index.
Identifiers: LCCN 2017031297 (print) | LCCN 2017045586 (ebook) | ISBN
  9781626177734 (hardcover : alk. paper) | ISBN 9781681035123 (ebook)
Subjects: LCSH: Amazon.com (Firm)--History--Juvenile literature. | Internet
  bookstores--United States--Juvenile literature. | Electronic
  commerce--United States--Juvenile literature. | Bezos, Jeffrey--Juvenile
  literature.
Classification: LCC Z473.A485 (ebook) | LCC Z473.A485 G74 2018 (print) | DDC
  381/.142--dc23
LC record available at https://lccn.loc.gov/2017031297

Text copyright © 2018 by Bellwether Media, Inc. PILOT and associated logos
are trademarks and/or registered trademarks of Bellwether Media, Inc.
SCHOLASTIC, CHILDREN'S PRESS, and associated logos are trademarks and/or
registered trademarks of Scholastic Inc., 557 Broadway, New York, NY 10012.

Editor: Betsy Rathburn   Designer: Josh Brink

Printed in the United States of America, North Mankato, MN.

amazon

Table of Contents

What Is Amazon?

Busy schedules often leave little time for shopping. Amazon can help! One afternoon, a family browses the company's web site. They choose backpacks, notebooks, and other school supplies. Someone needs soccer cleats. Amazon sells those, too! With the click of a button, the order is sent. In just a few days, the items arrive at their door. Amazon saved the family a lot of time!

Amazon.com, Inc. is one of the world's largest shopping web sites. Most people call it Amazon. Its company **headquarters** is in Seattle, Washington. Amazon sells a wide range of products. It is often called "the everything store." The company's **logo** is recognized around the world. It shows an arrow that stretches from the first A to the Z in the shape of a smile. Today, Amazon is one of the most successful Internet businesses in the world. The company is worth more than $400 billion!

By the Numbers

more than
45,000
robot workers in
Amazon Fulfillment
Centers

around
300 million
Amazon users

more than
300,000
employees

nearly
$136 billion
in sales in 2016

more than
250
Amazon Dash
Buttons available

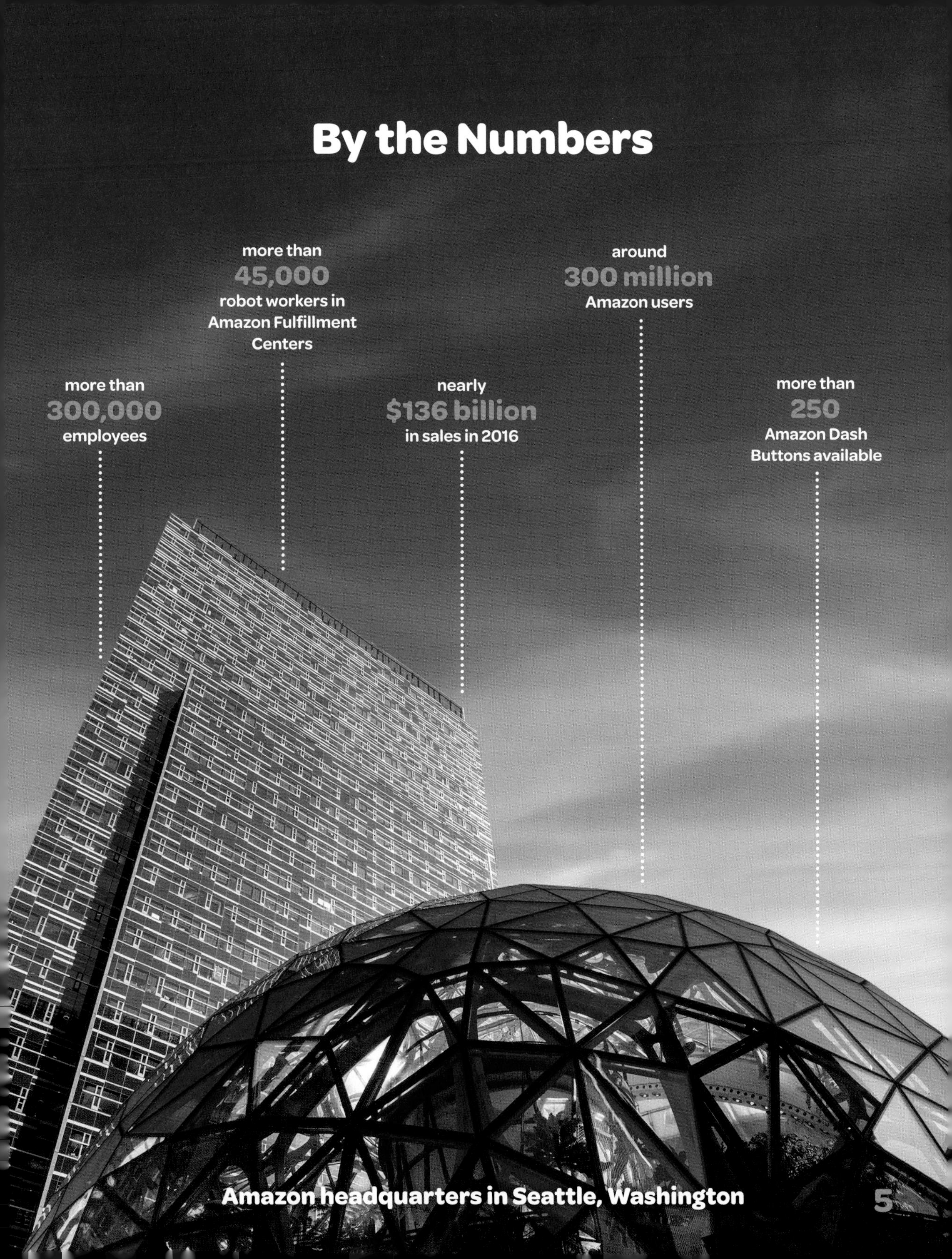

Amazon headquarters in Seattle, Washington

Jeff Bezos

Jeff Bezos founded Amazon.com in 1994. From a young age, Jeff enjoyed discovering how things worked. As a toddler, he tried to take apart his crib. When he was older, Jeff worked on science projects in his family's garage. He spent summers working on his grandfather's Texas ranch.

Jeff Bezos

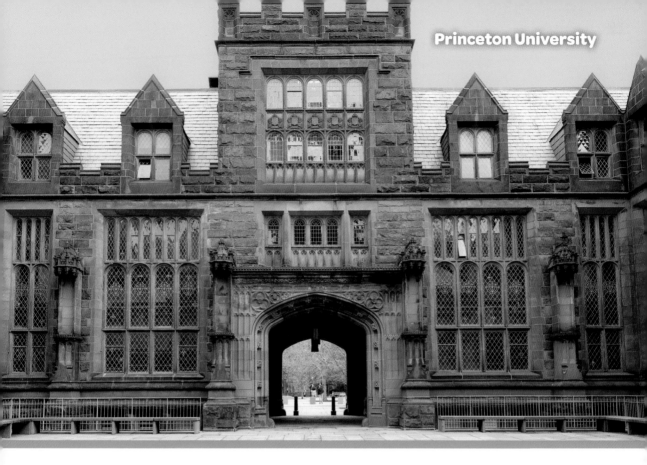

Jeff worked hard in high school, too. He excelled in math and science. He also became interested in computers. After graduating, Jeff attended Princeton University. There, he studied computer science and electrical engineering. Jeff graduated with high honors in 1986. He soon moved to New York City for work. At age 26, Jeff became a vice president at an **investment** company called D.E. Shaw. Two years later, he was the company's youngest senior vice president!

. . . .

A Big Dreamer

In high school, Jeff started an educational summer camp for younger students. It was called the DREAM Institute.

A New Idea

Few people used the Internet in the early 1990s. Even fewer businesses sold items online. Jeff saw a great opportunity. He left his job to start an Internet company. After considering several options, Jeff decided to sell books. They were easy to ship and in high demand. In 1994, Jeff moved to Washington to start the online bookstore. He named the company Amazon.com. Amazon offered one million book titles. Sales started on July 16, 1995.

Amazon was popular right away. In its first week, the company took $12,000 in orders! In its first month, Amazon filled orders from 45 countries and all 50 states. After only two years, Amazon became the first Internet store to have one million customers.

If Not Amazon...
Amazon was named after the Amazon River in South America. Other names in the running were Cadabra, Awake, and Browse.

Earth's Biggest Bookstore.

1990s tagline

9

The Everything Store

Amazon had a strong start but struggled to make a **profit**. Many business leaders doubted the company would last. But Jeff stayed patient. He believed success would come. His goals for Amazon went beyond books. He wanted the company to sell almost everything! Amazon began selling video games, DVDs, and CDs in 1998. It later added computer **software**, toys, tools, and other items. Shoppers around the world enjoyed the ease of shopping online. By the end of 2004, Amazon's sales had reached nearly $7 billion!

Amazon bookstore in Seattle, Washington

Brick And Mortar
Amazon is no longer just an online store. It has several bookstores across the country with more planned.

But Amazon did not stop there. In 2016, the company launched its own food **brand**. Wickedly Prime offers many food and drink choices. Customers love the brand's teas, soups, and healthy snacks. Shoppers can use Amazon to quickly get groceries and more!

One million titles, consistently low prices.

1990s tagline

Today, more than 180 million people browse Amazon each month. Customers choose from millions of new and used items. They even get product suggestions based on what they have bought in the past! When orders are placed, **fulfillment center** workers get them ready. They fetch, package, and mail the products. There are dozens of these centers around the world. Some centers even have robot workers!

Amazon Fulfillment Center in Peterborough, England

In the future, Amazon may have even more robot workers. The company is testing a new project that will speed up delivery for customers close to fulfillment centers. The tests use **drones** to deliver lightweight packages. The drones can hit speeds of up to 60 miles (96.6 kilometers) per hour. They can deliver products in 30 minutes!

Daily Workout

Amazon Fulfillment Centers are huge! Workers may walk between 7 and 15 miles (11.3 and 24.1 kilometers) a day while they are getting products.

Innovating Our Lives

Amazon is known for its **innovative** products and services. In 2005, the company launched a **subscription** service in the United States. It was named Amazon Prime. Over time, the service expanded to many other countries. Amazon Prime members pay a fee. This allows them to receive special services. Free two-day shipping is a popular Prime perk. In some cities, members can use Prime Now. Their orders arrive in two hours!

Prime members can also **stream** movies, music, and original programs. *Annedroids* and *Lost in Oz* are popular programs for kids. Around 80 million people in the United States enjoy the benefits of Amazon Prime.

Amazon creates many products, too. In 2007, the company released one of its most popular items, the Kindle. It was a handheld electronic book reader. Customers loved the idea of buying and downloading books on an electronic reader. In less than six hours, the Kindle sold out completely! It remained sold out for several months.

Never Run Out
Amazon Dash Buttons are devices that are connected to the Amazon store. Customers can use them to order regularly used items. When the button is pressed, Amazon sends the product!

Amazon Products and Services

Product	What Is It?	Launch Date
Prime	subscription service	2005
Amazon Video	Internet video on demand	2006
Kindle	e-reader	2007
Kindle Fire	tablet computer	2011
Kindle Paperwhite	e-reader	2012
Alexa	voice assistant	2014
Echo	Internet speaker system	2014
Prime Now	delivery service	2014
Amazon Fire TV	digital media player	2014
Dash Button	product ordering device	2015
Wickedly Prime	line of snacks and drinks	2016
Echo Dot	Internet speaker system	2016

Kindle Paperwhite

Dash Button

Echo Dot

Fire TV stick

The company **debuted** a device called Amazon Echo in 2014. Amazon Echo uses a voice assistant called Alexa. Alexa plays music and answers questions. It gives weather reports and delivers the news. People can ask Alexa to turn lights on and off and set alarms. They can even ask Alexa to order pizza! In cars, Alexa can give directions, start engines, and unlock doors.

Amazon introduces the Fire TV

Amazon Fire TV was also introduced in 2014. It is a box that connects televisions to the Internet. Owners use a menu to select TV programs, movies, **apps**, and games. Amazon Fire TV comes with an Alexa Voice Remote. People can ask Alexa to search for TV shows, movies, actors, and directors. Then Alexa finds results that match the requests!

Staying In Touch

Every employee at Amazon must spend two days every two years working at the customer service desk. Even Jeff Bezos takes a turn!

Making A Difference

Amazon is committed to making a difference in people's lives. Since 2013, the company has donated money to **charities** through the AmazonSmile program. Shoppers choose a charity when they buy items. Amazon then donates part of the sales to that charity. Over time, AmazonSmile has helped raise more than $60 million.

In 2016, Amazon started the Kindle Reading Fund. This program donates Kindle e-readers, Fire tablets, and Kindle e-books to schools and libraries that lack reading materials. These devices increase reading choices for people around the world.

Local Heroes
Amazon supports many projects in the Seattle area. The company built a neighborhood dog park and funds yearly fireworks. It even runs a free banana stand!

A BANANA A DAY KEEPS THE DOCTOR AWAY
TAKE ONE.
NOT JUST FOR AMAZONIANS, BUT FOR ANYONE IN THE COMMUNITY
ENJOY!

Amazon Go grocery store

Amazon continues to innovate, too. In 2016, the company began testing a new grocery store in Seattle. It is called Amazon Go. **Sensors** keep track of what customers buy and charge them automatically. In 2017, Amazon introduced the Dash Wand. This device lets shoppers order items using only their voice. Amazon continues to change how people live and shop!

Amazon Timeline

1994
Jeff Bezos starts Amazon.com

1998
Amazon starts selling CDs and DVDs

2005
Amazon Prime launches in the United States

1995
Amazon.com debuts on the Internet

2001
The company makes its first profit

1997
Amazon becomes the first Internet retailer to have one million customers

1999
Amazon expands into selling toys, electronics, and other products

2000
Amazon debuts the logo with an arrow running from the A to the Z

amazon Prime

2007
Amazon launches the
Kindle e-reader

2012
Amazon buys Kiva, a
robotics company

2015
First Amazon
bookstore opens
in Seattle

2017
Amazon buys
the Whole Foods
grocery store chain

2011
Kindle Fire tablet
debuts

2014
Amazon Echo
launches in the U.S.

2016
Amazon makes its
first drone delivery

Glossary

apps—small, specialized programs downloaded onto smartphones and other mobile devices

brand—a category of products all made by the same company

charities—organizations that help others in need

debuted—introduced for the first time

drones—aircraft that fly without pilots on board

fulfillment center—a place that stores, packages, and ships products

headquarters—a company's main office

innovative—introducing new ideas and methods

investment—money put into something with hopes that it will earn more money

logo—a symbol or design that identifies a brand or product

profit—money that is made in a business after all costs and expenses are paid

sensors—devices that detect and respond to signals

software—programs that tell a computer what to do

stream—to send or receive video from the Internet as a steady flow

subscription—an arrangement for regularly providing a service in exchange for money

To Learn More

AT THE LIBRARY

Green, Sara. *Jeff Bezos*. Minneapolis, Minn.: Bellwether Media, 2015.

Reeves, Diane Lindsey. *Find Your Future in Technology*. Ann Arbor, Mich.: Cherry Lake Publishing, 2017.

Sutherland, Adam. *Amazon: The Business Behind the "Everything" Store*. Minneapolis, Minn.: Lerner Publications, 2016.

ON THE WEB

Learning more about Amazon is as easy as 1, 2, 3.

1. Go to www.factsurfer.com.

2. Enter "Amazon" into the search box.

3. Click the "Surf" button and you will see a list of related web sites.

With factsurfer.com, finding more information is just a click away.

Index

The images in this book are reproduced through the courtesy of: Leonard Zhukovsky, front cover (Amazon gift card top left); Roman Tiraspolsky, front cover (Amazon books top left); Alexander Supertramp, front cover (Amazon cart icon top left); Teja Sv, front cover (phone top left); Keith Homan, front cover (boxes top center, blue gift card); josefkubes, front cover (logo top right); Jerek Kilian, front cover (blue Prime truck); rvlsoft, front cover (app icon); simone.brunozzi, front cover (green food bin bottom right); kativ, front cover (Kindle Fire bottom right); Maksim Kuzubov, front cover (hero computer); urbanbuzz, front cover (Fire Stick TV bottom left); Andriy Blokhim, front cover (green food bag bottom left); Genn Fleishman, front cover (Amazon paper bag bottom left); SEASTOCK, front cover (crown locker middle top), p. 11; James W Copeland, front cover (dash button top left), pp. 14, 15 (left middle); Ragilnih, title page; Jeramey Lende, pp. 4, 21 (bottom left); Dave Newman/ Alamy, p. 5; Chaiwatphotos, p. 5 (background); Dean Rutz/ Newscom, p. 6; Jay Yuan, p. 7; Hadrian, p. 8; Tom Bible/ Alamy, p. 9; Ted S. Warren/ AP Images, p. 10; Associated Press/ AP Images, p. 12; dpa picture alliance/ Alamy, p. 13; A. Aleksandravicius, pp. 15 (left), 21 (top left); Zapp2Photo, pp. 15 (right middle), 21 (bottom right); urbanbuzz, p. 15 (right); Senator2029, pp. 15 (bottom), 20 (bottom); McClatchy-Tribune/ Alamy, p. 16; Diane Bondareff/ AP Images, p. 17; Paul Christian Gordon/ Alamy, pp. 18, 19; Sarah2, p. 20 (top); Jonathan Weiss, p. 21 (top right).